Jane Grell is a teacher, poet and storyteller born on the Caribbean island of Dominica, living and working in London. She visits colleges, schools, libraries and community groups throughout the UK and abroad, enthralling children and adults of all ages and cultures.

She is an experienced INSET facilitator for teachers, demonstrating and encouraging the use of poetry and storytelling to develop literary creativity within the curriculum. She has contributed to Scholastic publications in both aural and written forms; she is also a frequent reviewer of their story and poetry books. A published poet, for both children and adults, her last poetry collection, White River Blues, was published in 2016.

Jane worked with BBC School Radio as an advisor on the multicultural content of its output, as well as presenting poetry and stories for its Primary Schools' Programmes.

About the illustrator

Jacqueline McFarlane is an East London based artist who has exhibited all over London in both solo and group shows. As well working as an illustrator, she also facilitates creative activity workshops for adults and children. Raised and educated in Hackney, Jacqueline worked for many years in the social care sector. In 2003, she completed a BA in Fine Art at the University of East London.

Mosquito Bounce
ONE

Mosquito One

Mosquito one, mosquito two
Mosquito jumps in the old man's shoe

Mosquito three, mosquito four
Mosquito opens the old man's door

Mosquito five, mosquito six
Mosquito picks up the old man's sticks

Mosquito seven, mosquito eight
Mosquito opens the old man's gate

Mosquito nine, mosquito ten
Mosquito bites the man again

For Rye Tafara and River Farai

two little bluebirds
soaring high
one named Tafara
one named Farai
fly Tafara
fly Farai
fly, fly
till you touch the sky

Little Red Monkey

little red monkey
sitting in a tree
little red monkey crouch
little red monkey hump
little red monkey scowl
little red monkey scratch, scratch, scratch

little red monkey
hanging from a branch
little red monkey swing
little red monkey grin
little red monkey spin
little red monkey jump, jump, jump

little red monkey
jumping to the ground
little red monkey bounce
little red monkey creep
little red monkey peep
little red monkey leap, leap, leap

little red monkey
up to mischief
little red monkey hip
little red monkey skip
little red monkey hop
little red monkey stop, stop, stop

little red monkey
and his tricks
little red monkey sing
little red monkey don't
little red monkey do
little red monkey boo
little red monkey shoo, shoo, shoo!

Nanny's Swivelling Chair

spin around
spin around
round and round
spin, spin
right off the ground
clickity-clackity
twist and twirl
plenty of spins
for an astronaut girl

spin around
spin around
round and round
spin, spin
right off the ground
clickity-clackity
ship ahoy
plenty of spins
for a sailor boy

At the Park

Swing low
Swing high
push me hard
till I touch the sky
take it gently
take it slow
please, one more push
before we go

Footprints

Footprints in the classroom
Footprints in the hall
But the footprints which I love the best
Are our footprints on the wall

Footsteps

footsteps on the ground
footsteps on the ground
tramp-tramp, tramp-tramp
what a lovely sound

footsteps in the street
footsteps in the street
trip-trip, trip-trip
oh so many feet

footsteps in the rain
footsteps in the rain
puddle-puddle, splash-splash
gurgling down the drain

footsteps in long grass
footsteps in long grass
swish-swish, swish-swish
move and let me pass

footsteps in the mud
footsteps in the mud
slip-slide, slip-slide
mind that tiny bud

footsteps up the stairs
footsteps up the stairs
tiptoe, tiptoe
make sure no one hears

footsteps in the dark
footsteps in the dark
woo-hoo-ooo, woo-hoo-ooo
what a ghostly bark

footsteps in my head
footsteps in my head
tikka-tokka, knock-knock
it must be time for bed

tikka-tokka*
tikka-tokka
knock-knock
TIME FOR BED!!!

*speed up

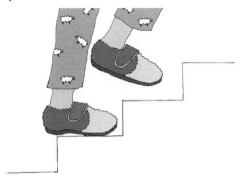

One Day, One Day – Konga Day

A call and response poem based on a Dominican
playground game. *'Konga Day'* is the response

one day, one day – *konga day*
I went to the forest – *konga day*
I saw a monkey – *konga day*
sitting up in a tree – *konga day*
he was eating bananas – *konga day*
and picking his nose – *konga day*

yes, eating bananas – *konga day*
while picking his nose
I said Mister Monkey
that's not very nice
eating bananas
and picking your nose

well that cheeky monkey – *konga day*
he jumped to the ground – *konga day*
looked me straight in the eye – *konga day*
and you know what he did?
he went rake-shake – *konga day*
he went raking-shaking – *konga day*

he went rake-shake – *konga day*
he went raking-shaking – *konga day*
one day, one day – *konga day*
in that very same forest – *konga day*
I spied Anancy – *konga day*
sleeping under a tree – *konga day*

yes, I spied Anancy – *konga day*
sleeping under a tree – *konga day*

I said, Brer Nancy, why you so lazy?
just sleeping all day, under mango tree
yes, sleeping all day, under mango tree

well that lazy spider – *konga day*
he jumped to his feet – *konga day*
looked me straight in the eye – *konga day*
and you know what he did?

he went rake-shake – *konga day*
he went raking-shaking – *konga day*
he went rake-shake – *konga day*
he went raking-shaking – *konga day*

Soggy Things

Puddle and splash
Puddle and splash
Together they go like bangers and mash

Rain and sun
Rain and sun
Put them together for rainbow fun

Frost and ice
Frost and ice
Winter's cold and not very nice

Sleet and snow
Sleet and snow
Inside houses
Lights all aglow

One March Day

milky sky
drifting snow
darkening clouds
sudden lightning
rolling thunder
biting winds
freezing rain
and then the sun came out

My Mum

my mum, she often talks in riddles
she'll say:
if you come to me with a bee in your bonnet
I'll send you away with a flea in your ear
just don't come to me with no bee in your bonnet
if you don't want a big, fat flea in your ear

but my gramps, he gives me a nice, big hug
and he says to mum:
you leave the child alone, you hear me?

My Pet

come sit with me and be my friend
I'll love you to the bitter end
I'll put up with your piteous pose
and even wipe your runny nose
I'll run a comb through your picky head
so natty, natty, natty dread
I'll scratch your back and call you poppet
my poor, poor pet

Chalk and Cheese

Mel and his brother are like chalk and cheese
chalk and cheese those two brothers are
if Mel is chalk and his brother cheese
you keep Mel and I'll have cheese please!

Our Class

Our class is a lot like that little girl
of nursery rhyme fame
I've forgotten her name
but you know the one
when she was good, she was very, very good
when she was bad, she was horrid
well, that's our class exactly

Our Teacher

Our teacher is batty
and looks quite a mess
but of all our school's teachers
we love him the best

Magical Bus Ride

sitting on the top deck
looking out the window
what do I see?
psychedelic slugs
sliding down a tree,
bursting into fountains
wonderful to see.

sitting on the top deck
looking out the window
what do I see?
two swans, red and blue
whizzing round a lake and singing
how do you do? how do you do? how do you do?

sitting on the top deck
looking out the window
what do I see?
a raft of hungry crocodiles
sharpening their teeth
and gliding towards me

sitting on the top deck
looking out the window
what do I see?
a band of dancing fireflies
doing the hokey-kokey
and hypnotising me

sitting on the top deck
looking out the window
what do I see?
why, it's your headteacher
riding on a donkey
and sipping a cup of tea

sitting on the top deck
looking out the window
what do I see?
a giant in his dressing gown
painting mini rainbows
all around our town

Sitting on the top deck
Looking out the window
What do *you* see?

Mosquito Bounce
TWO

Mosquito Bounce

two hungry mosquitoes sat on a fence
eyes popping
tongues lolling
just watching some children
watching some children
watching some children play
now they hadn't had a bite all day
they hadn't had a bite all day.

said the first mosquito to his friend on the fence
eyes popping
tongue lolling
I say, I haven't had a bite all day
haven't had a bite all day

the second mosquito just nodded his head
eyes popping
tongue lolling
he didn't have a word to say
as he hadn't had a bite all day
he hadn't had a bite all day

I know, said mosquito one, I've got an idea
let's read a poem to lure them here
if we want to have a bite today
if we want to have a bite today

a poem? non man, said mosquito two
this ain't no library
what's the matter wid you?

trust me, said his friend
I know children well
with a story or a poem
you could lead them to hell

go on then, said the other
try a poem lemme see
I'm feeling so hungry
I'll do anything for me tea.

well the first mosquito he cleared his throat, ahem!
to do a nursery rhyme which he knew by rote
to do a nursery rhyme which he knew by rote

mosquito one, mosquito two
mosquito jumps in the old man's shoe

mosquito three, mosquito four
mosquito opens the old man's door

mosquito five, mosquito six
mosquito picks up the old man's sticks

mosquito seven, mosquito eight
mosquito opens the old man's gate

mosquito nine, mosquito ten
mosquito now bites the man again.

the children took no notice and his friend
just laughed, kya, kya, kya, kya
then he said, Gimme de poem, lemme try it
my way
ah bet you dey listen to what I have to say
bet you dey listen to what I have to say.

The second mosquito he jumped off the fence
he limbered up his body which was taut and tense
I say he limbered up his body which was taut and tense.

(*Increase tempo*)

ah mosquito one,
ah mosquito two
ah mosquito jump in de ole man shoe

ah mosquito three,
ah mosquito four
ah mosquito open de ole man door

ah mosquito five,
ah mosquito six
ah mosquito pick up de ole man sticks

ah mosquito seven,
ah mosquito eight
ah mosquito open de ole man gate
ah mosquito nine,
ah mosquito ten
ah mosquito biting de man again.

well the children they came running
with a speed which was quite stunning
they laughed as they listened
then with pleasure they squealed
please, Mister Mosquito, do it again.
Oh Mister Mosquito, please do it again

they danced and they diddled
they frolicked and they fiddled
they chanted and they chiddled
then went home to their tea.

two miserable mosquitoes sat on a fence
wondering where they went wrong
they were so busy jiving they forgot to bite
and thanks to all their skiving, they faced a hungry night

and they never had a bite that day
no they never had a bite that day
they never had a bite that day

so next time two hungry mosquitoes you spy
desperately waiting to pounce
why not ask them to do
the Mosquito Bounce
just ask them to do
the Mosquito Bounce
don't forget now, ask them to join you in
the Mosquito Bounce!

ah mosquito one, ah mosquito two
ah mosquito jump in de ole man shoe...

Best Friends

Darius is my best mate
In the summer holidays
when he comes round for a sleep-over
he's always got his nose to the ground
looking out for tiny night creatures
through his binoculars

on the other hand,
I like to look up at the sky
and count the stars
through my telescope
I spot a trillion planets
and dream of flying into space

when dad comes to fetch us indoors,
he laughs and says
you are a funny pair, you two,
one's forever looking up
while the other's looking down.
when do you ever talk?

Darius and me,
we just roll our eyes
and say nothing
grown-ups
they just don't get it
do they?

Sing a Crooked Song

Han-a-lee and Han-a-brown
see the world from upside down
down side up and left side right
they really are extremely bright

Han-a-lee hails from the east
Han-a-brown comes from the west
when they meet, it's an enormous treat
to bow back to back, then clap their feet

Han-a-lee chews cups of tea
while Han-a-brown sips daintily
from a sulky Jaffa cake
which the cook forgot to bake

Han-a-lee and Han-a-brown
they take their porridge sitting down
one on a toadstool, one on a rack
both off the ledge of a railway track

Han-a-lee and Han-a-brown
view the world from down side up
they see what they like, love what they see
they really are a bit like you and me

so the next time you happen to look up a tree
you may very well see Han-a-lee
attempting to explode a frown
from off the nose of Han-a-brown

two cleverer girls I'm sure you'll agree
have never gone down in his-to-ry
since Han-a-lee and Han-a-brown
swapped a silly sixpence for a song

Come my Friend

you don't have to be good-looking to be my friend
you could be toothy and goofy
your knees knobbly and wobbly
your hair frizzy and natty, lanky and stringy
too fat, too short, too tall, too skinny
you'd still be my friend

you don't have to be clever to be my friend
you could be bumbling and fumbling
at times lazy and dozy
not confident and quick
but shy and even a bit thick
you'd still be my friend

you don't have to be cool to be my friend
you could be crazy and scatty
a tad moany and whiney
a big silly-billy
a right old wally
a bit of a fool to the rest of our school
you'd still be my friend

but what if you were a bully
all moody and mean
quite bossy and mouthy
your manners obscene
with a horrid little mind
not considerate nor kind
would you still be my friend?
I don't think so, do you?

Eva's Prayer

If I saw life through my mum's looking glass
I'd
eat all my greens
come top of the class
suck up to my teachers
be a sensible lass

take pride in my appearance
wear a smiley countenance
eat few chocolate chips
put no paint on my lips

wouldn't sulk, wouldn't scowl
be as sweet as a pea
a quite boring existence I'm sure you'll agree
not for me, no siree!

yet, just once in a while, I hope and pray
that mums are nearly as wise as people say
so the beautiful butterfly she sees in me
wriggling like mad to break free
could indeed become a reality
we'll see

My Granddad is a Saga-boy

my granddad is a boy
not a Rude-boy
nor a Teddy-boy
but a Saga-boy

he's great at cricket
ok at football
but it's when he dances
that everyone moves back
to form a ring around him
admiringly

his hair and clothes must be just-so
razor-sharp and smart
he never jumps around, my granddad
but just hugs me tight and slowly sways
to hot soca music
as if we were alone in the world
the two of us

my grandma pretends she's not impressed
but I can tell she is, when, trying to hide a
smile
she cheups and says to grandpa:
man, when you going to grow up, nuh
and stop playing Saga-boy?

my granddad, he just grins and winks at me
before closing his eyes
and stepping out with super-duper cool
when I grow up
I want to be a Saga-boy too
I really do

I Like You Gramps

I like you Gramps
because you're sweet
and if I were a bee
I wouldn't trade your love for honey

I like you Gramps
though without teeth
your little chats have got such bite
they lift and make my spirits soar
on golden wings like my best kite

I like you Gramps
though short of money
you always save a silver piece
to slip into my ready palm
when mum's not looking

I like you Gramps
because you're funny
and for those wrinkles peeking out
to tease a twinkle in your eye
be honest Gramps
do they know something I don't?

I like you best of all Gramps
for the stories you tell
the things you've seen!
the places you've been...

though I doubt just a little
I still quiver and tingle
from the ones which you tell
yes, the stories you *must* tell
with pleasure and over again

Nenen

I've got an aunty I call Nenen*
rosy and round
cashew-nut brown
sharp and so smart!
her walk is an undulating wave
her smile, from the gap in her teeth
a ray of morning sunshine

when she passes
grass bows respectfully
and even droopsy wayside flowers
does raise their eyelids high enough
to salute aunty Nenen as a woman of grit
yes mam
and so indeed do I

*Nenen, in Dominica means godmother

Living Libraries

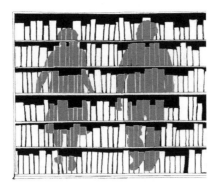

there's an old African saying
that when an old person dies
it is as if
a whole library has gone up in flames

I've got an itching left palm
my grandmother used to say
I will come into money, you mark my words
and somehow, she always did

she could forecast the weather too
my eyelids just dancing, dancing, all day long
plenty rain will fall tonight
and always came the cooling rains

on the subject of marriage, she was expert too
mind you don't be too choosey-choosey, you know
or you'll end up with jackass
prospective brides, be warned

mysterious
illogical
and with pots of wisdom to spare
let us keep alive their memories

Chatte pas la Watte ka baye Bal
(*When the cat's away, the mice play*)

chatte pas la, watte ka baye bal
the cat's away, rats are having a ball
grown-ups out
children having a whale of a time
under-twelves watching TV way past bedtime
teenagers throwing wild parties up so high
they even rock the sky

chatte pas la, watte ka baye bal
it's the same in any language
it's the same at any age
when the cat's away, the mice will play
mum's out, yippee!
no home cooking today
dad's phoning up for take-away
chatte pas la, watte ka baye bal

it's the same every time
it's the same in every way
is this Miss Johnson's class I hear?
I don't believe it!
she can't be in there
I knew it!

poor Miss Johnson's out with flu
and her supply teacher?
hot and bothered, his tie askew
I bet you he comes down with something too
if I told you once, I'll tell you again
chatte pas la, watte ka baye bal
when the cat's away, the mice, well...
they're bound to play, eh eh!

Petit Hache Ka Bat Gwo Bwa
Little Axe Chops Down Big Tree

petit hache ka bat gwo bwa	Little axe chops down big tree
cha, cha, cha	chop, chop, chop
petit hache ka bat gwo bwa	little axe chops down big tree
cha, cha, cha	chop, chop, chop
dit mwem, petit hache	tell me, little axe
dit mwem seegway ou, non?	tell me your secret, then?
coumen ou ca fer coupé	how can you cut down
gwo bwa cela	such a big tree
et ou say ani un petit hache?	and you just a little axe?
ah mais seegway mwem	my secret
say un seegway simple	is so very simple
ou kay taper y en twa ti bitens	it lies in three things
ki sa pwofiter ou aussi	which can work for you too
eben, dit mwem seegway ou, non	well, tell me your secret, then
ba mwem say twa bagailles cela	give me those three things
mwem besoin pour réussi	which I need to succeed
mandez n'emporte ti hache	ask any little axe and
y kay dit ou meme biten	she'll tell you the same
pièce twavaille en la ter	no task on earth
pas jamais twop gwo	is ever too great
si ou fait plan ou	all you need is planning
chember fort kon tétar	perseverance
et si ou twavaille avec courage	and courage

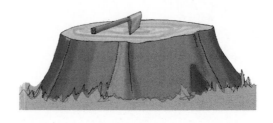

Acrostic Poem

Loving the power and the music of words

Introduction to people, their stories, their lives

Tucked up in bed with a book, sheer bliss!

Enjoying a poem, text message or joke

Releasing emotions along with deep thought

Always remembering to think what you write

Communicating simply and clearly

Yow, I'm talking about LITERACY!

A Good Book

A good book, like a reluctant dawn
can start off sluggishly
only to quicken as the drama unfolds.

It can be a conch shell, washed up on a beach
lifeless until picked up and held to the ear
unleashing an orchestra.

At times, it's like a rainbow
rising from a puddle on some busy city street
quite unexpected and so uplifting

A good book transcends time and place
magically speaking volumes
its power immense

Like a good teacher
it can crank your brain into gear
on a steel-grey morning, gently or otherwise

Like any granny
it has bags of common sense, life tips
and so much more besides

A good book is like popcorn munched at the cinema
whetting the appetite
only to leave you wanting more

It's like a Caribbean callaloo an' crab
with chewy bits that stick in your teeth
irritating, yet pleasurable

Or like jelly coconut water, slurped with eyes half closed
in the shade of a calabash tree
and tasting like heaven

It can be as reassuring as an old friend
with whom there is no need to speak
comforting even through silence

That good book, read under the covers
way past bedtime
with or without a torch
is wickedly appealing
whether you're ninety or nine.

Poetry Pepperpot

I was woken by a poem in the middle of the night
it poked with wordy fingers
and gave me quite a fright
an adjective peered in my face and said
she's sound asleep
an adverb leaned forward and pronounced:
actually, I'm not so sure
we'll soon find out piped up the verbs
as they bounced upon my bed.
one brazen hyperactive one even sat upon my head.

they counted all my fingers
there's one missing, they declared
one missing finger?
well, that was news to me, bad news indeed.
I sat up with an almighty lurch
and let out quite a screech

adverbs sidled sheepishly away
adjectives turned pale
superfluous words now quite confused
babbled a sorry tale

I scooped them up, the little scallywags
and stuffed them in my pepperpot
where awkward syllables are finely chopped
nouns picked and duly swallowed up
verbs prodded and unceremoniously dunked,
where wandering images are strip-searched
and left with little choice
but to be ingredients of my poem on the boil

Water Haiku

four fluffy cygnets
hitching a long, lazy ride
on mother swan's back

solitary shoe
on dark crest of river Thames
destiny unknown

river banks guarded
by ancient red-bricked buildings
stemming time and tide

in the Lake District
riding on an open bus
hooded mac pulled close

pleasure boats bopping
gawkily and self-conscious
like clumsy ducklings

Forest Haiku

twelve slender saplings
once planted in a circle
one enormous tree

the crunch-crunch of boots
echoing through the forest
on carpets of ice

the change of colours
every autumn's signature
steadfast stand the trees

moon-shadows humming
to early morning heartbeat
in time with the larks

wind, water, bird song
a cacophony of sound
that's Epping Forest

Wishful Thinking

If I couldn't be me
I'd most like to be a shower of tropical rain
Not the gentle sort which sprinkles the flowers
Or tickles your upturned face
But the pelting, chattering, noisy kind
That hammers on roof-tops in the dead of night

On the other hand, if I couldn't be me
I'd quite like to be an African talking drum
I'd rumble the secrets of the universe
and in a hundred different tongues
I'd beat out greetings across the land
JAMBO!
CA KA FET?
ASALAMALAIKUM!
HELLO!

But then again
If I couldn't be me
I'd as happily be a simple friendship song
with lots of notes, some high, some low
words full of cheer and hope
The most beautiful song I would surely be

And yet, the more I think about it
the clearer it becomes
that if I couldn't be me
I'd most certainly be
a shower of tropical rain
dancing from the tips of a banyan tree
to the tune of a song
from an old, old African drum

Possibilities

Once, I was a slimy maggot, the lowest living thing
Now, I am a blood-sucking leech, tenacious and life giving

Once, I was a puny earthworm, crawling on my belly
Now, I'm a boa constrictor, swallowing your telly

Once, I was a despised housefly, stuck in someone's soup
Now, I'm an admired butterfly, playing loop-de-loop

Once, I was an insignificant tortoise with eggshell eyes
Now, I am a flamboyant circus elephant in disguise

Once, I was a lonely mole, living down a dark, dark hole
Now, I'm a performing bear that flies in the air

Once, I was a lowly sparrow, hoppity-hopping down a grassy lane
Now, I'm a mighty eagle, soaring through clouds like an
    aeroplane

Once, I was an anxious, straight-laced, po-faced class-teacher
Now, I'm a cool, finger-snapping, toe-tapping, gum-chewing
    Ofsted inspector

Once, I was a ugly, ugly likkle dry up prune
Now, I'm a rosy mango by the light of a tropical moon

Once, I was a shy, shy picky-head gal
Now, I'm a poet, so please, may I be your pal?

Once, I lived on Dominica, where it rained and rained
Now, well now I live in England, so what's changed?

Voice from the Ghetto

When it's cold outside, this house cold
When it's raining outside, this house rain too
Whatever nature do, this house do
But that's where I live, that's my home

rage on chill winds
you don't scare this boy
strike up lightning, do your worst
he's not afraid
roll on thunder, if you must
you can't touch him
for has he not hoodwinked the drug pusher
the knife wielder, the gun-slinger
shut his flimsy door on violence
scorched dank depression to fan the flame of hope
swaddling himself
in the mantle of love which every so often
flickers in his grandmother's weary eyes?

the desert which surrounds him may be bleak
but the cooling draughts from his oasis
when it comes
will all the more sweetly quench his thirst

Dreaming for Change

I dreamt the world was a sea of plastic
plastic trees with plastic leaves
beneath which dry, plastic streams
shed silent tears

I dreamt I was a bird
stuck in a branch
with broken wings
dying

A fish swimming
against pollution's tide
fins torn
gasping

The last surviving earthworm
burrowing in vain for clean soil
shrivelling

I watched as every consumer item
slowly unwrapped
from its elaborate packaging

as fruit and vegetables
tumbled out of individual plastic bags
filling dustbins to overflowing
with no more room for household refuse
fast spilling onto every street
leaving the air, oceans, our planet
with such stench and horror
that I woke up convinced
there was no sense in sleeping
if I couldn't dream to change the world

Queen of the Night

I am lady moon, queen of the night
I glide around when the sun has gone
and all is still
I cast my fluorescent spell upon the trees
trickle my magical glow unto streams
and slipping through closed windows
I intrude on troubled dreams

A friend of graveyard folk
of ghosts and goblins
soucouyant and loupgaroo
of wandering spirits at the bewitched hour
I hold the secrets of knaves and lovers
who fear and love me in equal measure
I am lady moon, queen of the night

Bedtime

soft, fluffy eiderdown
warm sofa bed
plenty of pillows
to cushion my head

soft, fluffy eiderdown
enveloping me
like gently rolling waters
of the Caribbean sea

softly warm
      lapping waves
           dipping
                 down
                    deep into slumber land
                        of eiderdown
                              dreams.

Spaced Out

come fly with me
far above the clouds
way beyond the sky
further than the sun
floating
spinning
soaring high

come, we'll sip luminous droplets from the Milky Way
eat grated moon rocks sprinkled with star dust
from a silver tray
pull faces at the man in the moon
and tickle his beard with an asteroid spoon

come, we'll catch falling stars
and go to Mars, suspended from a comet's tail
we'll organise a moon-walking constellation
where we'll judge for shimmer, shine and glow
first prize will go to the one
who can glide like James Brown
light, graceful and super-slow

then when we've had our fill of space
we'll hitch a ride on a rollicking rocket
and blithely rejoin the human race.

My Neighbours

my neighbours are noisy, funny, wacky
and here's the proof:

It could have been thunder tiptoeing on roller blades across the sky
or a pair of talking drums rumbling out the latest village gossip
but no, it was only the Pettifers from number 9a
moving their furniture round – again!

It could have been an antique fire engine trundling down our road
or an enthusiastic dentist drilling till she dropped
but no, it was only sad Sabrina from over the road
practising on her violin while popping bubble gum

It could have been a couple of elephants stomping on our roof
or an army of bobbies pounding the beat
but no, it was only the Gurpalsinghs from upstairs
showing off their salsa dancing skills

It could have been a fast train hooting through a tunnel
or a hungry hyena coming face to face with his dinner
but no, it was only the reverend Bill from vicarage house
enjoying an hour of comedy on TV

It could have been one of the seven dwarfs prancing in fancy dress
or Anansi Spider twirling in Joseph's multi-coloured dream coat
but no, it was only Mr Ndusi from next door
shuffling off to his niece's wedding in Leytonstone

my neighbours, wacky, funny, noisy
come to think of it, I wonder what *they* think of me?

Walthamstow Market

people shopping
people walking
talking so loud in a surging crowd
Turkish, English, Patwa, Punjabi
Cockney, Ibo, Polish, Somali
all jostling for position in a spicy language callaloo.

people moving
people grooving
some of them skiving
more eyeing than buying
vendors busy selling and calling:
"Sweet mangoes, only two-fifty a box
come on girls, cheap tomatoes today
fifty P the lot
buy your bananaaas!"

stomachs rumbling
to smells of food tumbling
from trailers and cafes

stands and sidewalks;
fish and chips, jellied eels
rice an' peas, curry goat
onion bhajis, hot pakoras
codfish fritters, Johnny cakes
shish and doners, eggy noodles
Jamaican patties, Cornish pasties
there for the tasting
yours for the asking
washed down nicely with sorrel and ginger-beer
lassi or real ale;
take your pick, give yourself a treat
you'll need all your strength
to stay on your feet
as you mosey on down
London's longest market street.

people chatting
people laughing
easing down the high street
in tattoos and Mohicans
scarves and salwars
jeans and T-shirts
combats and baseball caps;
young ones, old ones
big ones, little ones
fat ones, skinny ones
black, brown and white ones
all on a bargain-hunting
cut-price seeking
culture-mixing
Walthamstow-lively market spree.

Freedom Wings

I got space to play the clown
worries never get me down
I got space between each pulse
so my heart can't play me false

from my head down to my toe
from my shoulder to elbow
I got space to fool around
with my feet still on the ground

I got space within my bones
not uptight like Mr Jones
lots of space to move my hips
dancing to my finger tips

I got space to laugh out loud
at times cry, why, I'm not proud
I got space to live my life
I got space to deal with strife

I got space to dream and love
thank my lucky stars above
I got space beneath my wings
I got wings to set me free

I'm so lucky to be me